PIONEER VALLEY EDUCATIONAL PRESS, INC

MOVING WEST

MICHÈLE DUFRESNE

TABLE OF CONTENTS

Heading West	2
Covered Wagons	6
Hard Work	8
Pioneer Children	12
Difficult Weather	16
New Towns	18
Glossary/Index	20

HEADING WEST

The first **settlers** arrived on the East Coast of America a few hundred years ago. As more and more people came, the cities and towns on the East Coast became crowded. People who worked in factories wanted to leave the cities. They wanted to have their own land so they could become farmers or ranchers, look for gold, or hunt and trade animal furs.

Back then, people could buy land out West for a very small price. Many people began to leave the cities and move west to start a new life. These people were called **pioneers**.

The trip out West was long and hard. There were dangers along the way as the pioneers traveled. They had to cross rushing rivers and face bad weather. Some people became ill.

Not everyone survived the trip.

➤ Some of the pioneers were freed or escaped slaves from the South. In many parts of the West, slavery was not allowed. Traveling there gave them a chance to begin a new life.

COVERED WAGONS

The first pioneers traveled west in wagons pulled by oxen or mules. The wagons were covered with cloth. They had large wheels that could roll over bumps in the trails.

People packed their belongings in the wagons. They took furniture and dishes and sometimes even pianos. They also packed dry foods that would stay fresh for a long time, like cornmeal, rice, and beans.

Sometimes they traveled with cows. The cows were used for milk or meat if the food ran out.

Children, old people, and sick people would ride in the wagon too. Everyone else had to walk.

HARD WORK

Living on the **frontier** was hard. There were many dangers and problems to be solved. Before planting crops, pioneers needed to clear their new land of trees and rocks. They also needed to build cabins or houses to live in.

Pioneer homes were built from logs that fit together without nails. A lot of the homes were small and simple with just one room. Everyone cooked, talked, and slept in the same space.

In some places, there were no trees to build houses with. On the prairie, people built homes out of **sod**. Sod is the top layer of the earth. It is made of grass, roots, and dirt. To make roofs, the pioneers used layers of brush, mud, grass, and sod.

Sod homes were not as strong as log homes. Bugs and mice could sneak in. Sometimes even snakes would slither into beds. A heavy rainstorm could make the roof fall in.

The pioneers also needed to build barns to keep their animals safe from wolves and other **predators**.

PIONEER CHILDREN

When pioneers first moved out West, there were no schools for children. As more people moved to an area, they would form a school. Most of the schools had just one room. One teacher would teach all of the grades. The children learned to read, write, and do math together. Instead of paper, the children wrote with chalk on **slates**.

Children only went to school in the winter and summer. In the fall and spring, they stayed home and helped with planting and harvesting crops.

Everyone in the family worked hard, even the children. They woke up early and worked from sunup to sundown. Even children who were only three or four years old had to help out. They would gather **kindling** for the fire, sweep the floor, and fetch water.

Older children did many of the same chores that grown-ups did. They hunted animals for food, milked the cows, and chopped wood for the fire. They took care of the babies, plowed the fields, and planted crops.

DIFFICULT WEATHER

Pioneers had to get used to different kinds of weather out West. In some places, the winter was much longer and colder than on the East Coast. It was hard to stay warm. Sometimes there were terrible **blizzards** that dumped enough snow to trap people in their houses.

Farmers often lost whole fields of crops to dust storms or tornadoes. Sometimes swarms of grasshoppers would eat all of the crops.

Long, hot summers made the grasses on the prairie dry. A flash of lightning could start a huge fire. It was hard to stop these fires from spreading and burning down the crops.

NEW TOWNS

At first, it was lonely on the frontier. People often lived far away from one another. But over time, more people began to settle out West. Homes, stores, churches, and schools were built. It was not long before the American West was filled with new towns.

Roads connected the new towns together. Railroad tracks made it faster, easier, and safer to travel west.

The pioneers of the past all had something in common: They wanted a better life. They were willing to take chances and leave their homes, friends, and family behind in order to find it.

Now that we have explored the West, where will the next pioneers travel? Maybe in the future they will fly to outer space, looking for a better life, just like the first pioneers!

GLOSSARY

blizzards: terrible snowstorms that go on for a long time

frontier: a distant area where few people live

kindling: dry things like twigs or papers that can be used to start a fire

pioneers: the first people to move to a new area

predators: animals that live by killing and eating other animals

settlers: people who move to a new area

slates: small sheets of rock that can be written on with chalk

sod: the upper layer of soil, which is made of grass and plant roots

INDEX

blizzards 16
crops 8, 13, 15, 17
East Coast 2, 16
frontier 8, 18
kindling 14
logs 9, 11
pioneers 3, 5, 6, 8, 10–12, 16, 19
prairie 10, 17
predators 11
railroad tracks 18
schools 12–13, 18
settlers 2
slates 12
slavery 5
sod 10–11
South 5
wagons 6–7
weather 4, 16
West 2–5, 12, 16, 18–19